£5.50

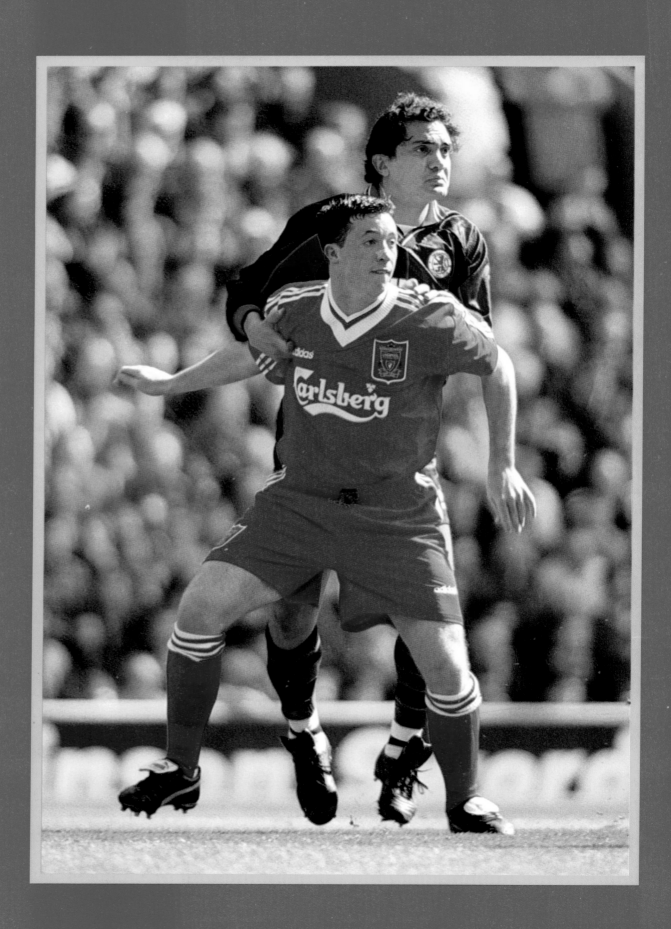

Believe me, you don't need much motivation when you play for Liverpool. Just pulling on that famous red shirt is motivation enough...Just walking out at Anfield beneath the famous sign above the tunnel is a great inspiration...Just listening to the roar of the Anfield crowd spurs you on. And when they sing 'You'll Never Walk Alone', well, it gets you right in the old heart strings.

I know all of that may sound like a load of footballing cliches, but they all happen to be true. Ask anyone at Anfield!

Everyone at the club hopes that you enjoy this, the second Official Liverpool Football Club Annual from Grandreams. It's crammed full of great stories from the 1995-96 season, profiles of Anfield's favourite players and tons of action packed photos...

Best Wishes,

Robbie Fowler

© 1996 Liverpool Football Club

Written by Tony Lynch
Photographs by John Cocks
Designed by Dave Saunders

All facts believed correct at the
time of going to press

Published by Grandreams Ltd
Jadwin House
205-211 Kentish Town Road
London NW5 2JU

Printed in Belgium

Contents

LIVERPOOL FC factfile

Address: Anfield Road, Liverpool L4 0TH

Telephone: 0151-263 2361
Ticket information:
0151-260 9999
Fax: 0151-260 8813

Current Ground Capacity: 41,000
Pitch Size: 110 x 74 yards

Chairman: DR Moores
Chief Executive/General Secretary: Peter B Robinson
Commercial Manager: Mike Turner
Director of Youth: Steve Heighway
Sponsors: Carlsberg

Team Manager: Roy Evans
Assistant Manager: Doug Livermore
Coach: Ronnie Moran
Physio: Mark Leather

Nickname: The Pool
Team Colours: All red
Second Strip: Green and white shirts, green shorts, green/white socks

Record Attendance: 61,905 v Wolverhampton Wanderers, FA Cup Fourth Round on 2.2.1952

Record League Victory: 10-1 v Rotherham Town, Second Division on 18.2.1896

Record Defeat: 1-9 v Birmingham City, Second Division on 11.12.1954

Record Cup Victory: 11-0 v Stromsgodset Drammen, European Cup-Winners' Cup First Round first leg on 7.9.1974

Most League Goals in a Season: 106, Second Division on 1895-96

Most Individual League Goals in a Season: 41, by Roger Hunt in 1961-62

Most League Goals in Aggregate: 245, by Roger Hunt between 1959-1969

Most League Appearances: 640, by Ian Callaghan between 1960-1978

Record Transfer Out: Ian Rush to Juventus for £2.75 million

Record Transfer In: Stan Collymore from Nottingham Forest for £8.5 million

LIVERPOOL FC
Roll of Honour

LEAGUE CHAMPIONS
- 18 TIMES
1900-01, 1905-06, 1921-22,
1922-23, 1946-47, 1963-64,
1965-66, 1972-73, 1975-76,
1976-77, 1978-79, 1979-80,
1981-82, 1982-83, 1983-84,
1985-86, 1987-88, 1989-90

LEAGUE CHAMPIONSHIP
RUNNERS-UP – 10 TIMES
1898-99, 1909-10, 1968-69,
1973-74, 1974-75, 1977-78,
1984-85, 1986-87, 1988-89,
1990-91

SECOND DIVISION CHAMPIONS
– 4 TIMES
1893-94, 1895-96, 1904-05,
1961-62

FA CUP WINNERS
– 5 TIMES
1965, 1974, 1986, 1989, 1992

FA CUP RUNNERS-UP
– 5 TIMES
1914, 1950, 1971, 1977, 1988

LEAGUE CUP WINNERS
– 5 TIMES
1981, 1982, 1983, 1984, 1995

LEAGUE CUP RUNNERS-UP
- TWICE
1978, 1987

EUROPEAN CUP WINNERS
– 4 TIMES
1977, 1978, 1981, 1984

EUROPEAN CUP
RUNNERS-UP
– ONCE
1985

UEFA CUP WINNERS
– TWICE
1973, 1976

EUROPEAN CUP-WINNERS CUP
RUNNERS-UP – ONCE
1966

YOU'LL NEVER WALK ALONE

LIVERPOOL
FOOTBALL CLUB

EST. 1892

LIVERPOOL in 1995-96

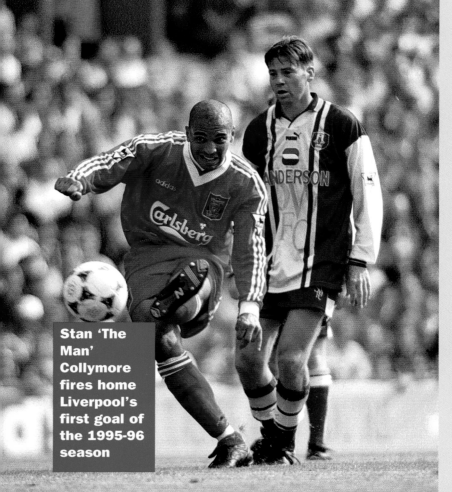

Stan 'The Man' Collymore fires home Liverpool's first goal of the 1995-96 season

Having tasted success in the 1995 Coca-Cola Cup, in which they beat Bolton Wanderers 2-0 in the Wembley final, Anfield's mix of young stars and experienced veterans were anxious for more glory in 1995-96 – both on the domestic scene and in Europe.

The Reds' Premiership campaign kicked-off at Anfield on 19 August, with the visit of SHEFFIELD WEDNESDAY. New signing Stan Collymore really made it a red-letter day for himself and for the club, by netting the only goal of the game. It was a truly spectacular strike, hit from all of 25-yards and involving some neat footwork by 'Stan the Man'.

What a great start!

Anxious faces on the Liverpool bench in the match against Leeds

**A Macca
Attack
against
Leeds**

Two days later, the Reds travelled to Elland Road to take on LEEDS UNITED in a virtual heatwave. This was another game settled by a single, spectacular goal. But unfortunately it was scored by Leeds' brilliant Ghanaian international Tony Yeboah!

Things got back on track in a big way in the Reds' third game of the season, away to TOTTENHAM HOTSPUR. Liverpool were magnificent, classy and clinical as they cruised to a 3-1 victory, with John Barnes scoring twice and Robbie Fowler volleying home his first goal of the campaign after a typical Liverpool build-up. Spurs 'new-boy Chris Armstrong replied for the home side, but the Londoners were well beaten.

**Neil
Ruddock
scores
the
winner
against
QPR**

Robbie
Fowler,
surrounded
by Rangers!

**The Reds -
flat out in
celebration**

Neil Ruddock was one of the the heroes of the night in Liverpool's next home game, against QUEENS PARK RANGERS under the Anfield floodlights. His low hard drive in the 30th minute, ended in the back of Tony Roberts' net for the only goal of the game. The other hero was Rob Jones, who cleared an almost certain QPR goal off the line late in the game.

The three points gained took Liverpool's tally to 9 from four games, and saw them laying third in the Premiership table behind Newcastle and Leeds.

RUBBLE RAISER!

Around £200,000 was generated for charity, when souvenirs made from the rubble of Anfield's famous Kop went on sale in August!

MATCH FAX - AUGUST 1995

Competition	Date	Venue	Attendance	Result
Prem	19.8	Anfield	40,535	Liverpool 1 Sheffield Wed 0
Prem	21.8	Elland Rd	35,852	Leeds Utd 1 Liverpool 0
Prem	26.8	White Hart Lane	31,254	Spurs 1 Liverpool 3
Prem	30.8	Anfield	37,548	Liverpool 1 QPR 0

Super REDS

ROB JONES

PHIL BABB

LIVERPOOL in 1995-96

International priorities meant that Liverpool were not in action again until Saturday 9 September - an away visit to WIMBLEDON. Despite creating a great many scoring opportunities, the Reds were unable to find the net. And disaster struck in the 28th minute when the Dons' Ray Harford scored from a free-kick taken by Andy Thorn. It was the only goal of the game.

On 12 September Liverpool began their UEFA Cup adventure with a First Round first leg visit to SPARTAK VLADIKAVKAZ in Russia. And it turned out to be a most satisfactory trip on with goals from Steve McManaman and Jamie Redknapp wiping out the early lead taken by the home side, and a healthy 2-1 advantage to carry into the home leg.

Four days later saw Liverpool's magnificent destruction of reigning Premier League champions BLACKBURN ROVERS, at Anfield. Jamie Redknapp was first off the mark, on 12 minutes, when he smashed a shot past Tim Flowers from all of 20 yards.

Ten minutes later Robbie Fowler was on target for his second goal of the season, a brave diving header which connected with a cross from Rob Jones. Stan Collymore also struck his second of the campaign, on 29 minutes, a stunning 30-yarder that curled around Flowers in the Rovers' goal. The match ended at 3-0, a and was the Reds' most impressive performance of the season to date.

September

Jamie opens the scoring against Blackburn

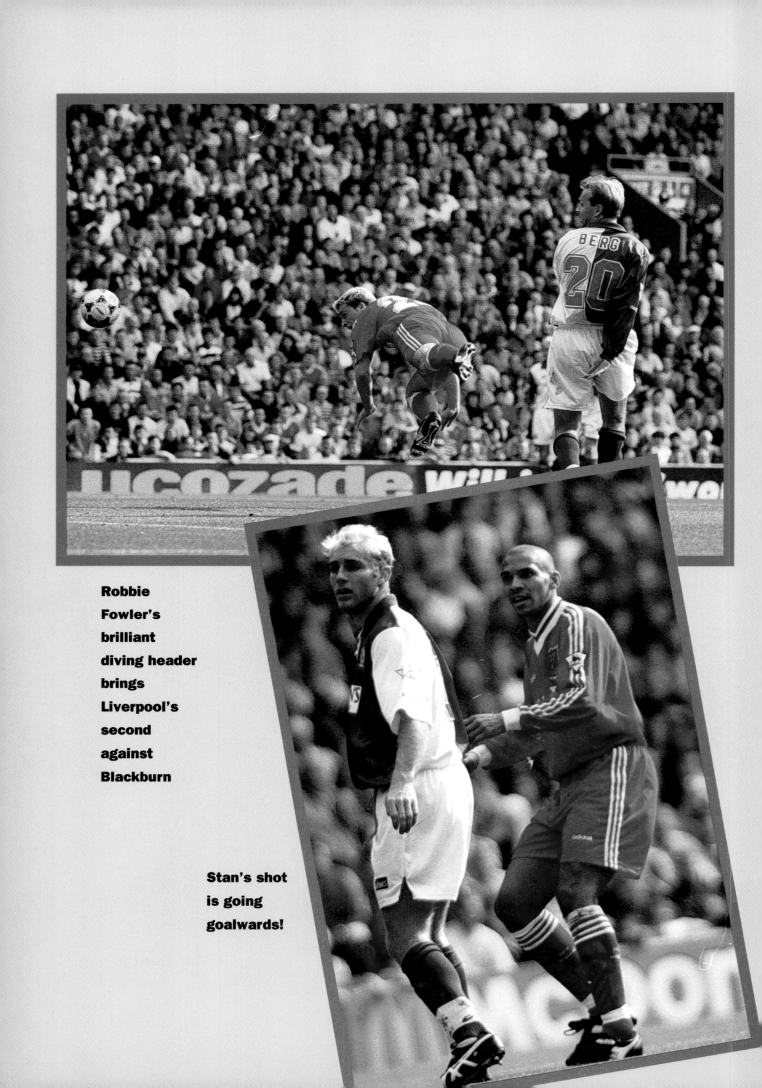

Robbie
Fowler's
brilliant
diving header
brings
Liverpool's
second
against
Blackburn

Stan's shot
is going
goalwards!

Macca opens the scoring against Sunderland

First Division SUNDERLAND were the next visitors to Anfield, in the first leg of the Second Round of the Coca-Cola Cup. The Reds' first defence of the trophy they won in 1994-95 proved a tricky game, with the Rokerites almost scoring from the penalty-spot – except for a magnificent save by David James.

In the end Liverpool won 2-0 with terrific goals by Steve McManaman (9 minutes) and Michael Thomas (73 minutes).

On the following Saturday Premiership newcomers BOLTON WANDERERS came to Anfield, anxious to climb out of the danger zone at the foot of the table. But Liverpool did them no favours, instead they dished out a harsh lesson in the realities of life in the Premier League.

Robbie Fowler, in particular, was absolutely magnificent. The Anfield Ace scored no less than four times (twice in the first half, twice in the second) – and then Steve Harkness rounded off the afternoon with Liverpool's fifth late in the game.

Bolton had enjoyed a late surge to hit two goals of their own through Andy Todd and Mark Patterson, but the 5-2 scoreline was an accurate representation of the game.

Red-Hot Robbie in devastating action against Bolton

Robbie gets to keep the matchball!

Michael Thomas in UEFA Cup action.

Liverpool's fourth home game on the bounce, saw the visit of SPARTAK VLADIKAVKAS to Anfield in the second leg of the UEFA Cup First Round tie. The Reds, intent on protecting that 2-1 lead from the away leg, defended well under presssure and eventually produced a 0-0 draw. The only sour note of the evening was a booking for Neil Ruddock, his second in the competition, which meant he would miss the first game of the next round against Brondby through suspension.

September closed with Liverpool through to the next round in Europe and sitting fifth in the Premeirship with 15 points from seven games. Newcastle, Villa Manchester United and Leeds occupied the first four places, in that order.

TOP FANS

Did you know...Liverpool's fans were voted the best behaved supporters in the country!

MATCH FAX - SEPTEMBER 1995

Competition	Date	Venue	Attendance	Result
Prem	9.9	Selhurst Park	19,530	Wimbledon 1 Liverpool 0
UEFA Cup	12.9	Vladikavkaz	38,000	Spartak Vladikavkas 1 Liverpool 2
Prem	16.9	Anfield	39,502	Liverpool 3 Blackburn 0
Coca-Cola	21.9	Anfield	25,579	Liverpool 2 Sunderland 0
Prem	23.9	Anfield	40,104	Liverpool 5 Bolton W 2
UEFA Cup	26.9	Anfield	35,042	Liverpool 0 Spartak Vladikavkas 0

Super Saver DAVID JAMES

Liverpool's Number One is among the best keepers in the country and a real favourite with the Anfield crowd.

Born in Welwyn Garden City in August 1970, he started out as a schoolboy training with Spurs, but he became a trainee with Graham Taylor's Watford and eventually turned pro in January 1988.

Four years later – after success in the FA Youth Cup and some 88 appearances for the Hornets – he was regarded as the hottest young keeper around and was snapped up by The Reds for around £1 million.

But it took David a while to gain a regular place in the Liverpool first team – in those days the Number One jersey seemed to be the exclusive property of a certain Bruce Grobbelaar!

But these day, there's no doubt who is first choice between the sticks at Anfield. And surely it can't be long before David is considered for international duty, having already played at 'B' and Under-21 levels for England.

FACT FILE
Name: David Benjamin James
Birthdate: 1 August 1970
Birthplace: Welwyn Garden City
Height: 6' 5" Weight: 14st 5lbs
Previous club: Watford
International: England 'B', Under-21

Another great save from Dee Jay!

The outgoing David James stands tall in the Liverpool goalmouth

17

LIVERPOOL in 1995-96

Robbie Fowler chips Peter Schmeichel for Liverpool's second goal against Manchester United

Liverpool kicked-off October with a Premiership visit to Old Trafford. This was the game in which Eric Cantona made his return for MANCHESTER UNITED, following his long suspension. Within a minute the French maestro had made his mark on the match by providing the pass from which the unmarked Nicky Butt opened the scoring for United.

Robbie Fowler equalised on 32 minutes with a thunderous shot from 18-yards, after Jason McAteer had set up the chance. Robbie was on target again in the 53rd minute when he put Liverpool ahead with a tremendous chip shot which beat Peter Schmeichel.

But it was Eric Cantona who was to have the final say in the match. He scored United's equaliser from the penalty-spot after Jamie Redknapp was adjudged to have fouled Ryan Giggs in the box. The points were shared, the honours even.

Next came the visit to SUNDERLAND for the second leg of the Coca-Cola Cup First Round tie. The first half was marred by the sending-off of Rob Jones, in an incident for which he later apologised, describing it as 'my worst moment since I've been in the game'. He was later suspended for three matches. The result itself was settled by a Robbie Fowler goal on the half-hour, which gave the Reds a 3-0 aggregate victory and a place in the Third Round.

More international action interrupted the Premiership programme and The Reds did not play again until 14 October. Ron Atkinson's COVENTRY CITY were the visitors and they put in a fine performance to go home with a 0-0 draw in the bag. The Sky Blues were the first club to take any points off the Reds at Anfield in 1995-96.

Steve McManaman is tackled in the match against Coventry

Ian Rush scores his 48th League Cup goal

On 17 October Liverpool faced the tough test of an away match in the UEFA Cup Second Round against Danish club BRONDBY. In what was the Reds' 160th Euro game they emerged with a creditable 0-0 draw to take back to Anfield for the next leg. The defence, Mark Wright in particular, were in fine and disciplined form.

After the trip to Denmark it was back to Premiership action for the Reds on the following Sunday with a visit to SOUTHAMPTON at The Dell. The Saints began well with a goal headed by Gordon Watson after just three minutes. But the visitors were soon in command, with Steve McManaman easily earning his the Man of the Match honours by scoring twice in Liverpool's 3-1 victory. Jamie Redknapp added the third late in the game.

The next match at Anfield saw Coca-Cola Cup Third Round action against MANCHESTER CITY. It was a close game throughout the first half as Liverpool clung on to a 1-0 lead, gained with a 9th minute strike by John Scales.

The City defence did not give way again until Robbie Fowler scored in the 74th minute to put the Reds two-up. Five minutes later Ian Rush scored his first goal of the season - and his 48th in the League Cup, which put him within one goal of the tournament record held by Geoff Hurst. A fine evening's work was then rounded-off by Steve Harkness on 82 minutes for a 4-0 victory and a place in the Fourth Round.

19

Robbie Celebrates!

Four days later MANCHESTER CITY were once again the visitors to Anfield, in the Premiership. And this time they had even less luck!

In form Ian Rush was the first on target, with a goal on the rebound after just three minutes. Three minutes after that, Jamie Redknapp scored and Liverpool went in at half-time with a 2-0 lead.

But it was the Reds' second half performance that was to be the talk of the Premiership. Just two minutes after the restart Robbie Fowler got his name on the scoresheet, after losing two City defenders and hitting home from close range. Neil

Ruddock got in on the act with a goal headed in from a Jamie Redknapp corner, to make the score 4-0.

But there was still more to come from the Rampant Reds. On the hour Robbie Fowler got his second of the game after converting a Jason McAteer shot. Not to be outdone, Ian Rush capped the afternoon's entertainment with his second goal, on 64 minutes.

Jamie Redknapp gets in a shot against Manchester City

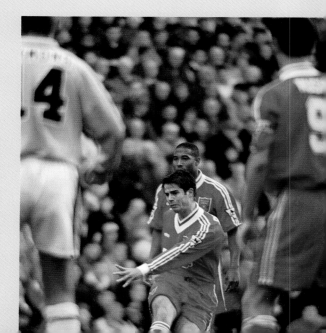

The 6-0 victory kept third placed Liverpool in touch with the Premiership leaders Newcastle United and Manchester United. The Anfield Reds now had 23 points from 11 games.

After those high notes, October was destined to end on a definite low, with the visit of BRONDBY for the UEFA Cup Second Round second leg match. Despite the advantage of having a 0-0 aggregate at home, Liverpool allowed the tie to slip away with a 1-0 defeat.

The deciding goal, a header by Dan Eggen from a corner, came late in the second half and completely crushed Anfield's Euro hopes for the season.

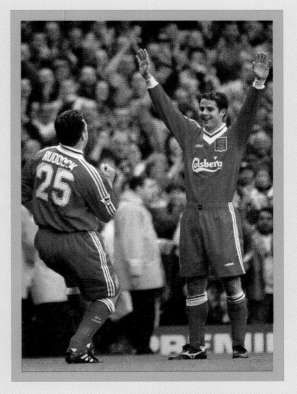

Neil Ruddock and Jamie Redknapp celebrate Liverpool's fourth goal against Manchester City

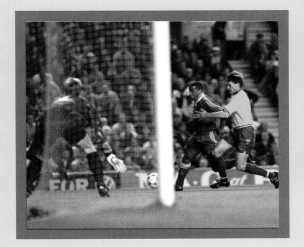

John Barnes attacks the Brondby goal, but Liverpool exit from Europe

Mark Wright on the attack against Brondby

MATCH FAX - OCTOBER 1995

Competition	Date	Venue	Attendance	Result
Prem	1.10	Old Trafford	34,934	Man. Utd 2 Liverpool 2
Coca-Cola	4.10	Roker Park	20,560	Sunderland 0 Liverpool 1
Prem	14.10	Anfield	39,079	Liverpool 0 Coventry City 0
UEFA Cup	17.10	Brondby	37,648	Brondby 0 Liverpool 0
Prem	22.10	The Dell	15,245	Southampton 1 Liverpool 3
Coca-Cola	24.10	Anfield	29,394	Liverpool 4 Manchester City 0
Prem	28.10	Anfield	39,267	Liverpool 6 Manchester City 0
UEFA Cup	31.10	Anfield	35,878	Liverpool 0 Brondby 1

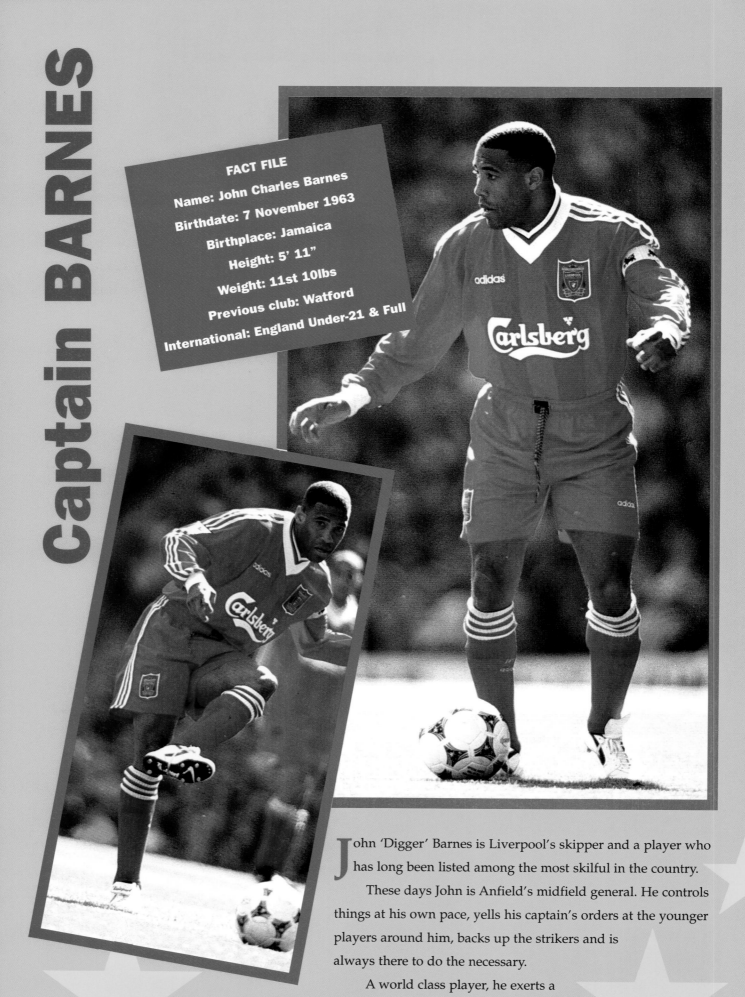

Captain BARNES

FACT FILE

Name: John Charles Barnes

Birthdate: 7 November 1963

Birthplace: Jamaica

Height: 5' 11"

Weight: 11st 10lbs

Previous club: Watford

International: England Under-21 & Full

John 'Digger' Barnes is Liverpool's skipper and a player who has long been listed among the most skilful in the country.

These days John is Anfield's midfield general. He controls things at his own pace, yells his captain's orders at the younger players around him, backs up the strikers and is always there to do the necessary.

A world class player, he exerts a positive influence throughout the team.

LIVERPOOL in 1995-96

November began with another jolt for Liverpool. In their toughest league clash of the season so far, the team travelled to St James Park to take on table-toppers NEWCASTLE UNITED.

Managed by former Anfield favourite Kevin Keegan, the Magpies had been the Premiership's pace-setters throughout the season so far, and were determined to wipe out memories of what had been a promising run in 1994-95 – a run that had eventually petered-out in frustration and a 6th place finish.

Liverpool were top dogs for 99% of the match, even though Les Ferdinand had opened the scoring for the home side in the second minute. Ian Rush redressed the balance eight minutes later with a relatively easy goal from a deflected ball. From then on the Reds took control.

Kevin Keegan later said that he would have been happy to settle for a draw. But he was obviously relieved that three points were in the bag for Newcastle. The killer blow had come in injury time when a mistake by David James was clinically punished by Steve Watson. The defeat pushed Liverpool down to fifth place, and increased Newcastle's lead at the top to 5 points.

That mind-blowing result at Newcastle was the prelude to a disastrous run for the Reds. In the next Premiership clash, against neighbours EVERTON at Anfield, on 18 November (international action had once again interrupted the Premiership programme), Liverpool went down 2-1.

The damage was done via a fine performance from The Toffees' Andrei Kanchelskis who chose this match to score his first goals for his new club. They both came in the second half and gave the Blues control. Robbie Fowler pulled one back for the Reds with two minutes to go, but by then it was too late.

Later, team boss Roy Evans described the result as a 'big blip for us'. The 'blip' took the Reds down to seventh place in the table.

Ian Rush goes up against Everton's Dave Watson

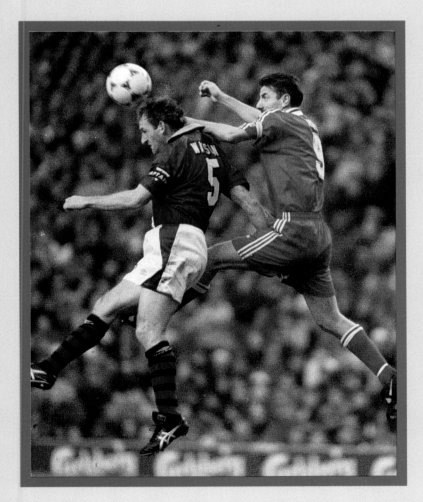

Macca tries to break through against Everton

Robbie scores for Liverpool, but can't prevent the 'big blip'

Four days later Liverpool were in East London for the Premeirship clash with WEST HAM UNITED. It was a thrilling match, full of end-to-end play and incidents galore. Yet, when referee Winter blew the final whistle the scoreline remained at 0-0. The game was notable for the return to action of Stan Collymore, replacing the injured Ian Rush.

In their next match Liverpool were stunned by an early goal scored by MIDDLESBROUGH's Neil Cox at the Riverside Stadium. It was a setback from which they never really recovered. Even when Neil Ruddock headed an equaliser in the 62nd minute, 'Boro replied within 60 seconds through Nick Barmby. And the scoreline remained at 2-1 for the remainder of the match. It was Liverpool's fifth Premiership defeat of the campaign.

November closed as it had begun, with a defeat by NEWCASTLE UNITED,

this time in the Coca-Cola Cup Fourth Round, at Anfield. Again it was Steve Watson who scored the winning goal, on 77 minutes – a clever chip over David James. Liverpool were out of the competition, and a miserable month was over. Things just had to improve...

Kevin Keegan - an old friend returns to Anfield

Jason McAteer puts the block on Darren Peacock

Stan leaps over Newcastle's Shaka Hislop

MATCH FAX - NOVEMBER 1995

Competition	Date	Venue	Attendance	Result
Prem	4.11	St James'	36,547	Newcastle 2 Liverpool 1
Prem	18.11	Anfield	40,818	Liverpool 1 Everton 2
Prem	22.11	Upton Pk	24,324	West Ham 0 Liverpool 0
Prem	25.11	Riverside	29,390	Middlesbrough 2 Liverpool 1
CCC 4 Rd	29.11	Anfield	40,077	Liverpool 0 Newcastle 1

Super REDS

NEIL RUDDOCK

FACT FILE
Name: Neil Ruddock
Birthdate: 9 May 1968
Birthplace: Wandsworth
Height: 6' 2" Weight: 12st 12lbs
Previous clubs: Millwall (twice),
Tottenham Hotspur (twice), Southampton
International:
England Youth, 'B', Under-21 & Full

JOHN SCALES

FACT FILE
Name: John Robert Scales
Birthdate: 4 July 1966
Birthplace: Harrogate
Height: 6' 2" Weight: 12st 7lbs
Previous clubs:
Bristol Rovers, Wimbledon
International: England 'B' & Full

LIVERPOOL in 1995-96

Stan equalises against the Saints

SOUTHAMPTON were the first visitors to Anfield in December, and they opened the scoring after an hour of play, with a Neil Shipperley header from a Jason Dodd cross. Seven minutes later John Barnes set-up Stan Collymore whose shot produced the equaliser. The scoreline remained at 1-1.

At last things began to look up when the Reds beat BOLTON WANDERERS at Burnden Park, their first win in seven games. The result was decided by the only goal of the match, scored by an in-form Stan Collymore, his second goal in successive games. Stan pounced on a defensive error before netting past keeper Keith Branagan on 61 minutes. The three valuable points lifted Liverpool from 8th to 6th position in the Premiership table.

28

Stan does
it again -
against
Bolton!

Robbie about to fire home his second goal against Manchester United

Christmas comes early to Anfield!

Sunday 17 December brought an early Christmas present to Liverpool when they beat second placed MANCHESTER UNITED at Anfield. It was a marvellous performance by the Reds, who were once again showing their true class.

Robbie Fowler scored twice. His first came just before half time, from a free-kick some 25-yards out which he curled around Peter Schmeichel in United's goal. His second, three minutes from time, was hit from close range after a great pass from Steve McManaman. Another marvellous result followed with ARSENAL's visist to Anfield two days before Christmas, and super striker Robbie Fowler was once again the star of the show.

Ian Wright opened the scoring with a penalty for the Gunners after just eight minutes; he had been fouled by Mark Wright.

Robbie's first goal came five minutes before the break, an 18-yard shot which sailed into David Seaman's net. On 59 minutes he collected a Stan Collymore header and fired home from the edge of the penalty-area. Collymore again provided the pass from which Fowler struck his third goal of the game in the 78th minute. It was the second time that Robbie Fowler had scored a Premiership hat-trick against Arsenal.

Liverpool were due to meet Aston Villa at Villa Park on Boxing Day, but just two hours before kick-off time, the game was postponed due to a frozen pitch. Roy

Robbie Fowler on his way to a second hat-trick against the Gunners

Evans was furious at the late decision to cancel, and he was especially disappointed for those Liverpool fans who had travelled all the way to Birmingham to watch the match. He said: 'My staff went to the ground at ten o'clock to put out the kit, and there was absolutely no hint that the game was in danger. I find it astounding that a Premeirship match can be called off so late in the day.'

Liverpool were not in action again until 30 December

Robbie celebrates his third goal against Arsenal

with their Premiership visit to CHELSEA. The Blues were in good form, scoring first with a marvellous John Spencer volley on nine minutes. The shot gave David James no chance.

Twenty-five minutes later Liverpool fashioned an equaliser from a short corner which was nudged on by Jason McAteer to Steve McManaman who volleyed home to bring the Reds back into the match. A minute before half time John Spencer finished of a marvellous individual run to restore Chelsea's lead.

In the second half Chelsea were punished for sitting back and defending their slender lead. Eventually Liverpool's pressure paid off with Steve McManaman's second goal of the game, on 76 minutes, from a Stan Collymore pass. The points were shared.

Liverpool's improved form throughout December saw them rising to third place in the Premiership table at the year's end, with 35 points from 20 matches. Everyone at Anfield was looking forward to 1996...

Robbie is presented with the Man of the Match Award - but who's the fellow in Red?

MATCH FAX - DECEMBER 1995

Competition	Date	Venue	Attendance	Result
Prem	2.12	Anfield	38,007	Liverpool 1 Southampton 1
Prem	9.12	Burnden Pk	21,042	Bolton W 0 Liverpool 1
Prem	17.12	Anfield	40,546	Liverpool 2 Manchester Utd 0
Prem	23.12	Anfield	39,806	Liverpool 3 Arsenal 1
Prem	30.12	Stamford Bdg	31,137	Chelsea 2 Liverpool 2

Liverpoo

FC 1995-96

LIVERPOOL in 1995-96

Stan scores Liverpool's third against Forest

The New Year began brilliantly for Liverpool, with a 4-2 home defeat of NOTTINGHAM FOREST. It was a remarkable game, made all the more remarkable by the Reds' comeback from a 2-0 deficit. England international Steve Stone had opened the scoring for Forest on 12 minutes, and their lead had been increased by Ian Woan five minutes later. It looked as though Forest were heading for their first victory at Anfield in 26 years.

Liverpool had it all to do – and they did it in style.

On 31 minutes Robbie Fowler pulled one back with a header from a Stan Collymore cross. Nine minutes later the same combination resulted in Fowler's equaliser, another header. The Reds took command from then on and Stan Collymore deservedly put them ahead on 61 minutes when he pounced on a defensive error to score. Forest's miserable afternoon was completed three minutes from time when the unfortunate Colin Cooper deflected a Collymore pass beyond Mark Crossley's reach.

The Third Round of the FA Cup saw Liverpool drawn to play at home to ROCHDALE. Unfortunately for the Third

It's all over for Forest as Colin Cooper's own goal goes in

The Reds celebrate their succesful fightback against Forest

in a minute to give the home side a 3-0 lead.

Three minutes into the second half Rochdale's Peter Valentine steered a Jason McAteer cross past his own keeper Chris Clarke. Ian Rush got in on the act in the 62nd minute when he blasted the Reds fifth goal past Clarke. It was an historic strike, marking Ian's 42nd FA Cup goal and breaking the record previously held by Denis Law.

In the 70th minute Robbie Fowler provided Stan Collymore with the pass from which Stan struck his second goal of the game. Jason McAteer made it 7-0 with four minutes to play. Liverpool had blasted their way into the Fourth Round draw.

Division club, this was to be the exact opposite of a 'giant-killing'.

The Reds were rampant – Robbie Fowler began the rout in the 21st minute with an excellent shot from 15-yards. As the half time whistle loomed Stan Collymore struck twice

Rushie the record breaker!

35

Rushie saves the day!

Hillsborough was the venue for Liverpool's return to Premiership action on 13 January. SHEFFIELD WEDNESDAY, eager to wipe out that first day of the season defeat at Anfield, scored after just seven minutes. Darko Kovacevic put the finishing touch to a great move down Liverpool's right flank.

Wednesday held on their lead until, with just three minutes left, substitute Ian Rush saved the day for the Reds with a terrific shot which was deflected past keeper Chris Woods. Result: 1-1.

On 20 January the Anfield faithful were treated to a vintage Liverpool performance against LEEDS UNITED. Neil Ruddock opened the scoring after 25 minutes when he headed home a great cross from Rob Jones. At half-time the scoreline stood at 1-0, and no-one was expecting the magical soccer that was to follow in the second period.

On the hour Robbie Fowler hit home from the penalty-spot after Gary Kelly had fouled Rob Jones. Seven minutes later Robbie was on target again when, from just two yard out, he converted a Stan Collymore pass into Liverpool's third goal of the game.

Stan Collymore got in on the act two minutes from time, with a magnificent right foot drive from all of 25 yards. Then in the last minute Neil Ruddock wrapped it all up when he scored from close range after a Jason McAteer corner. The stunning 5-0 victory gave the Reds championship challenge a marvellous boost.

The Reds' good work continued with their visit to ASTON VILLA on the last day of January. Under the Villa Park floodlights Liverpool left it late to edge ahead in a game which they controlled from the kick-off.

It was Stan Collymore who opened the

door in the 62nd minute, when he unleashed a powerful right-footed drive after receiving a short ball from a John Barnes free kick. Three minutes later Robbie Fowler struck his 21st Premiership goal of the campaign after a great build-up involving Steve McManaman and Jason McAteer.

The 2-0 victory edged Liverpool into second place in the Premiership table.

Neil Ruddock head his first goal against Leeds

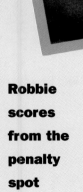

Robbie scores from the penalty spot

MATCH FAX - JANUARY 1996

Competition	Date	Venue	Attendance	Result
Prem	1.1	Anfield	39,206	Liverpool 4 Nottingham F 2
FAC 3rd Rd	6.1	Anfield	28,126	Liverpool 7 Rochdale 0
Prem	13.1	Hillsborough	32,747	Sheffield Wed 1 Liverpool 1
Prem	20.1	Anfield	40,254	Liverpool 5 Leeds United 0
Prem	31.1	Villa Park	39,332	Aston Villa 0 Liverpool 2

The REDS' Strike Force

23+8= a great strike force

FACT FILE
Name: Stanley Victor Collymore
Birthdate: 22 January 1971
Birthplace: Stone
Height: 6' 4" Weight: 13st 1lb
Previous clubs: Wolves, Crystal Palace,
Southend United, Nottingham Forest
International: England Full

FACT FILE
Name: Robert Bernard Fowler
Birthdate: 9 April 1975
Birthplace: Liverpool
Height: 5' 8" Weight: 11st 8lbs
Previous club: None
International:
England Youth, 'B', Under-21 & Full

The two players took a while to get their double act together. But once they had learned one another's game, there was no stopping them. Between them they scored 42 Premeirship goals last season.

There will be many more to come from the Reds' latest Strike Force...

Robbie Fowler - the Toxteth Tornado, and a player developed from a very young age through Liverpool's excellent youth system...

Stan Collymore - £8.5 million worth of striking talent who honed his skills in the lower divisions and burst to prominence with Nottingham Forest...

Together they form Liverpool's lethal strike force, one that is feared by defences up and down the country.

After enjoying a fabulous season in 1994-95, in which he became the Reds' top scorer with 25 Premiership goals, Robbie Fowler found himself competitng for a place in the Liverpool line-up at the start of the 1995-96 campaign. The reason? The arrival of Stan Collymore.
Robbie relished the sitation.
'Obviously Stan's arrival means I've got to fight for my place,' he said.
'But I can handle it. I've got a new five year contract and I intend to honour it.'
That turned out to be good news for Liverpool fans everywhere.

LIVERPOOL in 1995-96

February

Mark Wright heads clear against Spurs

February's action began with the visit to Anfield of high-flying TOTTENHAM HOTSPUR, an exciting team equipped with a strong strikeforce in Teddy Sheringham and Chris Armstrong, and a team who had been keeping pace with the Premiership front-runners.

Yet, despite the tremendous fire-power available to both sides, no goals were forthcoming and the points were shared.

On 7 February bad weather put paid to Liverpool's FA Cup Fourth Round tie at Shrewsbury. This meant the next time the Reds saw action was on the 11th at QUEENS PARK RANGERS. On 15 minutes Mark Wright, hovering on the edge of the area, collected the ball as it rebounded out of

defence, and he fired home a terrific shot to give Liverpool the lead.

Fifteen minutes later Robbie Fowler made it 2-0 after connecting with a long pass from Stan Collymore. Robbie slipped the ball beyond Jurgen Sommer in Rangers' goal then followed it up into the net.

In the second half QPR looked the better team, as Liverpool's concentration seemed to wander a bit. Daniele Dichio fired in a 35-yarder on 66 minutes. The ball struck Phil Babb and was deflected into David James' net. After that Liverpool put in some serious defending to hold on to the three points.

On 14 February everyone at Anfield, every Liverpool fan and every follower of football was saddened by the news that former manager Bob Paisley had died.

Phil Babb takes care of things

Tributes to the great man poured in and the club gates were adorned with flowers and wreaths in his memory. A minute's silence in memory of Mr Paisley was observed before the rearranged SHREWSBURY v Liverpool FA Cup tie on the morning of 18 February.

On a muddy pitch Liverpool dominated the Second Division side for most of the match. The first goal came after seven minutes from Stan Collymore who collected a Steve McManaman pass before hitting an under-powered shot which just managed to trickle across the goal-line before keeper Paul Edwards could catch up with it!

Liverpool's second was a long time coming, and it came courtesy of an own goal by Shrewsbury's central defender David Walton on 69 minutes, when he fluffed a clearance from a Phil Babb header. Six minutes later Robbie Fowler got his name on the scoresheet when he capitalised on a defensive error, rounded the goalkeeper and slotted home.

Stan can't believe he's scored!

The Reds' fourth came from Jason McAteer - his second for the club - when he put the finishing touch to a great move involving Stan Collymore and Steve McManaman. Liverpool were through to the Fifth Round when they would meet Charlton Athletic.

It was off to Ewood Park on 24 February for the Premiership clash with BLACKBURN ROVERS. Liverpool's opening goal was the most freakish of the whole season. It happened in the 10th minute when Stan Collymore struck a none to forceful shot towards the Blackburn goal. Keeper Tim Flowers had it covered and would easily have gathered the ball - if it hadn't struck a divot in the pitch and skewed its way past him and into the net. Collymore was a surprised as Flowers, but the Liverpool man was the one with a smile on his face.

Eleven minutes later, Stan the Man struck again. This time with en expertly struck free kick, which beat Tim Flowers

from all of 25 yards. Rovers pulled one back with a Jason Wilcox header on 26 minutes.

The Reds went 3-1 ahead in the 70th minute through Michael Thomas, who pounced on a brilliant Robbie Fowler through ball to slot home past Flowers. Once again Blackburn responded by scoring one of their own, by Tim Sherwood on 83 minutes, during a goalmouth scramble. But that was the last goal of the afternoon and the points went Liverpool's way.

Michael Thomas hits the Reds' third goal

Liverpool's last match in February was the FA Cup Fifth Round tie against CHARLTON ATHLETIC from the First Division. It proved to be a tough match for the Reds, as Charlton were a highly skilful and competitive outfit.

Robbie Fowler struck first with a marvellous glancing header from a Jason McAteer cross on 12 minutes. The ball skimmed past Charlton keeper Mike Salmon and the Liverpool team breathed a collective sigh of relief at having made the vital breakthough.

Liverpool's second came almost on the hour. Michael Thomas flew down the right flank before crossing the ball for Stan Collymore to supply a wonderful finish from 11 yards.

The Reds appeared to be in control now, and a place in the Sixth Round looked a certainty. But then Charlton pulled one back through Kim Grant with just two minutes left on the clock. After that the Londoners pummelled the Reds' defence and earned a couple of corners, as they fought for the equaliser. Thankfully, Liverpool held on - but only just.

Robbie's glancing header agaiinst Charlton

John Barnes heads away

Mark Wright's goal against QPR on 11 February was his first in three years! Stan Collymore's freak goal against Blackburn on 24 February could make a great 'What Happened Next?' poser in some future edition of A Question of Sport!

On 22 February, Liverpool midfield ace Jan Molby left Anfield to become player/manager of troubled Swansea City. Jan, a Danish international, had been with Liverpool for almost twelve years.

BOB PAISLEY OBE 1919 - 1996

Bob Paisley, English football's most successful manager, was born on 23 January 1919. He began

Tributes from both halves of Merseyside

with the famous amateur club Bishop Auckland and collected an Amateur Cup winners' medal in 1939, before joining Liverpool. The war delayed his league

debut until the 1946-47 season in which Liverpool won the Championship. In 1950, after scoring in the FA Cup semi-final against Everton, he was disappointingly dropped from the Liverpool side for the final against Arsenal, and the FA struck a special losers' medal for him.

After retiring in 1954 he was persuaded to join the Anfield coaching staff. He later became assistant to Bill Shankly and the legend of the Anfield 'Boot Room' began. After playing

an important role in the rise of the Reds, he was chosen as Shankly's successor in 1974.

Few would have predicted that this quiet, unassuming man would set Liverpool on the road to becoming the most successful English club of all time - but under Paisley the Reds won the Championship six times, the League Cup three times, the European Cup three times, the UEFA Cup once, the European Super Cup once and the Charity Shield six times.

He was voted Manager of the Year a record six times, was awarded the OBE in 1977, the Freedom of the City of Liverpool and a PFA Merit Award in 1983 – the year of his retirement. Bob passed away on 14 February 1996.

The one minute silent tribute in memory of Bob Paisley before Liverpool's FA Cup tie at Shrewsbury

MATCH FAX - FEBRUARY 1996

Competition	Date	Venue	Attendance	Result
Prem	3.2.	Anfield	40,628	Liverpool 0 Spurs 0
Prem	11.2	Loftus Rd	18,405	QPR 1 Liverpool 2
FAC 4th Rd	18.2	Gay Meadow	7,752	Shrewsbury 0 Liverpool 4
Prem	24.2	Ewood Pk	30,895	Blackburn 2 Liverpool 3
FAC 5th Rd	28.2	Anfield	38,818	Liverpool 2 Charlton Athletic 1

It's MACCA!

Macca beats Gary Pallister to the ball at Wembley

FACT FILE

Name: Steven McManaman

Birthdate: 11 February 1972

Birthplace: Bootle

Height: 5' 11" Weight: 10st 2lbs

Previous club: None

International: England Youth, Under-21 & Full

Steve McManaman is a wonderful player, full of skill, speed, enterprise and that essential enthusiasm which all the great footballers share.

He is also an unpredictable player - defenders don't know which way he will go, and it must terrifying having to face up to him.

Last season Steve was given licence to roam, in a 'free' role for Liverpool. It suited him down to the ground and Robbie Fowler claimed that his good friend created two-thirds of Liverpool's goals.

To have a player like Macca around, is like gold-dust to any club.

Super REDS

DOMINIC MATTEO

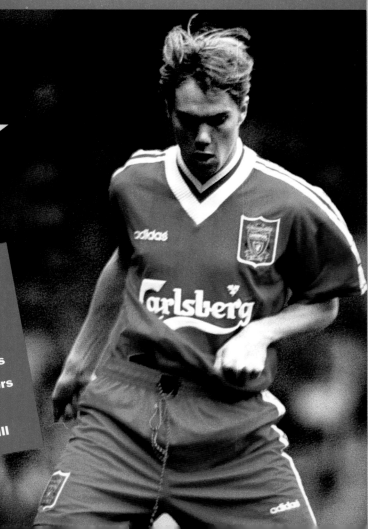

FACT FILE
Name: Dominic Matteo
Birthdate: 28 April 1974
Birthplace: Dumfries
Height: 6' 1" Weight: 11st 8lbs
Previous club: Sunderland (loan)
International:
England Youth & Under-21

JASON McATEER

FACT FILE
Name: Jason Wynn McAteer
Birthdate: 18 June 1971
Birthplace: Birkenhead
Height: 5' 9" Weight: 11st 5lbs
Previous club: Bolton Wanderers
International:
Republic of Ireland 'B' & Full

LIVERPOOL in 1995-96

One... Two... Three... and there's only seven minute gone against Villa!

ASTON VILLA were the first visitors to Anfield in March - and within seven minutes of the kick-off they were three goals down! The Liverpool onslaught started after barely a minute had ticked by, when Steve McManaman swiftly finished off a move involving John Barnes and Stan Collymore.

Hot-Shot Robbie Fowler was on the scoresheet two minutes later, after slipping past Steve Staunton, and firing home a rocket-shot from all of 30-yards. It was Fowler's turn again in the seventh minute when he put the finishing touch to a pass supplied by Rob Jones.

After such a blistering start the Reds inevitably slowed down. But Villa did not really get a look in for the rest of the game, the scoreline remained the same and the three points were in the bag. It was Liverpool's sixteenth game unbeaten.

It was FA Cup action next, in Liverpool's Sixth Round encounter with LEEDS UNITED on 10 March at Elland Road. It was a game dominated by defensive tactics, frayed nerves and a lot of tension. Despite the Reds going close through Steve McManaman and Robbie Fowler, the match ended with an almost inevitable 0-0 scoreline and the prospect of a tough replay back at Anfield.

Super Steve fires in the first against Wimbledon

A hard fought Premier League encounter with WIMBLEDON was played out at Anfield on 13 March. Liverpool should have won the match, but a seemingly legitimate goal by Michael Thomas was ruled offside by the linesman (Robbie Fowler had also had a goal disallowed earlier in the game).

The Reds did score twice, through Steve McManaman and Stan Collymore, but the Dons got two of their own, via Efan Ekoku and Dean Hodsworth, and the points were shared.

The result, while extending Liverpool's Premiership run to 14 unbeaten league games, actually put a dent in the title challenge. The Reds needed to get back to winning ways - and fast!

Glenn Hoddle's CHELSEA came to Merseyside on 16 March in the Premiership and were seen by 40,820 spectators, Anfield's biggest crowd of the season. They saw the Reds extend that unbeaten run to fifteen Premiership games.

The match was evenly balanced throughout the first half, although McManaman and Collymore both went close for Liverpool.

The deadlock was broken early in the second period when Mark Wright popped up to head home a John Barnes cross. And the points were sealed in Liverpool's favour by none other the Robbie Fowler, with another of his expert glancing headers - this time from a well-judged cross from the right by Jason McAteer. It was Red-Hot Robbie's 30th goal of the season in all competitions.

The Reds had found their way again.

It's no use arguing, Steve!

Robbie heads home

LEEDS UNITED came to Anfield on 20 March for the FA Cup Sixth Round replay - and they met with a Macca-Attack! Super Steve was in tip-top form as he ducked and weaved his way through the Leeds defence throughout the second half and took pot-shot after pot-shot. His first goal came on 57 minutes, after collecting a pass from Rob Jones and unleashing a blistering left foot drive which beat John Lukic in the Leeds goalmouth.

Macca was on target again 16 minutes later, this time after a tantalising one-two with Robbie Fowler. Robbie wrapped things up on 81 minutes with a curling, left-footed, free kick hit from all of 25-yards, to make the final scoreline 3-0 to the Reds.

Liverpool throughly deserved their place in the FA Cup semi-final.

After the Cup glory, came a setback in the Premiership with the visit to NOTTINGHAM FOREST on 23 March. This match marked Stan Collymore's first return to the club he had left in the summer - and the Forest fans gave him all sorts of stick. Despite Stan's best efforts the hostile atmosphere affected his game and he was substituted by Ian Rush with 20 minutes remaining.

By then Liverpol were 1-0 down, to a Steve Stone goal scored just before half time, and Forest had shut up shop. The scoreline remained the same.

It was Liverpool's first defeat since

Magnificent Macca scores in the FA Cup Sixth Round replay against Leeds...

...That's Macca's second!

Robbie hits home his free kick to make it 3-0 to Liverpool

Fowler's second came four minutes from time, when he latched on to a weak clearance by the Villa defence and hammered home a left footed half-volley. Then in the last minute of the game, Jason McAteer made it 3-0 with low shot from a Steve McManaman cross.

Liverpool had booked a place in the FA Cup final and would face Manchester United who had defeated Chelsea 2-1 in the other semi-final at Villa Park.

November, and it did Anfield's title hopes no good whatsover.

March ended on a high note for Liverpool, with the FA Cup semi-final defeat of ASTON VILLA at Old Trafford. The Man of the Match was Robbie Fowler, who had made his full England debut four days earlier. Robbie scored twice - to keep up his record of scoring in every round so far.

The first goal came from a Jamie Redknapp cross. Robbie produced one of his trademark glancing headers to put the ball in the bottom corner of Mark Bosnich's net.

Robbie's diving header opens the scoring in the FA Cup semi-final against Aston Villa

MATCH FAX - MARCH 1996

Competition	Date	Venue	Attendance	Result
Prem	3.3	Anfield	39,508	Liverpool 3 Aston Villa 0
FAC 6th Rd	10.3	Elland Rd	24,632	Liverpool 0 Leeds 0
Prem	13.3	Anfield	34,063	Liverpool 2 Wimbledon 2
Prem	16.3	Anfield	40,820	Liverpool 2 Chelsea 0
FAC 6th Rd Rep	20.3	Anfield	30,812	Liverpool 3 Leeds 0
Prem	23.3	City Ground	29,058	Nottingham F 1 Liverpool 0
FAC SF	31.3	Old Trafford	39,072	Aston Villa 0 Liverpool 3

Redder's RETURN

It was great to see the return to action of Jamie Redknapp late last season, after he had been sidelined for four months with a hamstring injury sustained while on duty for England.

So impressive was he on his return for the Reds, that England coach Terry Venables included him in the squad for the Euro 96 Championships.

Venables, who knows a thing or two about footballers, had nothing but praise for the young Liverpool midfielder and even compared him to a young Paul Gascoigne at his best - and we all know how good *he* is!

Roy Evans was delighted too, and said that having Jamie back was like signing 'a new, quality player'.

Super REDS

MARK KENNEDY

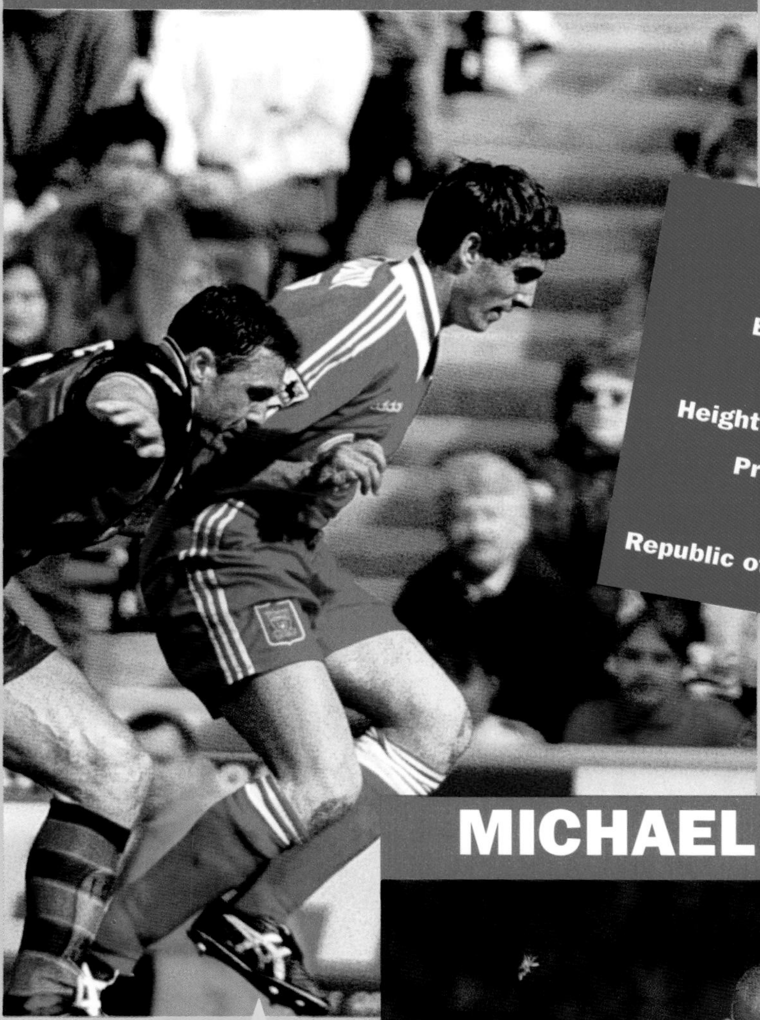

FACT FILE
Name: Mark Kennedy
Birthdate: 15 May 1976
Birthplace: Dublin
Height: 5' 11" Weight: 11st 9lbs
Previous club: Millwall
International:
Republic of Ireland Youth & Under-21

MICHAEL THOMAS

FACT FILE
Full Name: Michael Lauriston Thomas
Born: Lambeth, 24 August 1967
Height: 5' 10" Weight: 12.4st
Previous Clubs: Arsenal, Portsmouth (loan)
International: England Full,
'B', Under-21, Youth & Schools

LIVERPOOL in 1995-96

Robbie gets in a shot against Newcastle

Stan Collymore equalises for the Reds

A pril 3 brought arguably *the* finest match of the season. It was played at Anfield and Liverpool's opponents were fellow title contenders NEWCASTLE UNITED. Both sides desperately wanted to win this match. Both needed a positive result to stay in touch with league leaders Manchester United.

The drama was set-up early on, when Robbie Fowler headed home a left-sided cross from Stan Collymore after just two minutes. Eight minutes later Newcastle's own hot-shot, Les Ferdinand, equalised with an unstoppable shot that beat David James.

Four minutes after that, the Magpies went ahead, when French ace David Ginola took on a Ferdinand through ball, out-ran Jason McAteer and fired home.

Twelve minutes into the second half Robbie Fowler evened things up with his second goal of the game, a low, hard drive from the egde of the area, which had been set up by a McManaman pass. The Reds' joy was short-lived, however, as the classy Colombian Faustino Asprilla fired Newcastle back in front three minutes later.

Next, it was Stan Collymore's turn to supply an equaliser after another ten minutes or so of frenzied action. Stan got between two Newcastle defenders to fire home Jason McAteer's cross. It now looked for all the world as if the points would be shared - and indeed that might have been a fair result.

But there was more drama to come, and it arrived in the last minute of this pulsating game. Stan

Neil Ruddock clears from defence

Collymore was the hero with a rocket-like left footed shot that won the game after some neat approach work by John Barnes and Ian Rush.

It had been a classic match and a wonderful advertisement for Premier League football.

And it kept the title race wide open.

After the euphoria of the victory over

Stan Collymore shoots Liverpool's first goal against the Hammers

Newcastle, came the disappointment of defeat at COVENTRY CITY, and the tragedy of Steve Harkness breaking his leg in a tackle with John Salako.

The only goal of the game came in the 17th minute, from Coventry's Noel Whelan who converted a Peter Ndlovu cross.

It was most definitely a below par performance by Liverpool, against a Coventry side battling in the releagation zone and desperate for points. The normally reliable Robbie Fowler had the opportunity to level things up in the last minute, but his shot went straight into the arms of keeper Steve Ogrizovic.

Afterwards Roy Evans questioned whether the referee had allowed enough

injury time. The result certainly dented the Red's title chances.

Two days later WEST HAM UNITED came to Anfield, for Liverpool's fourth important match in the space of nine days. This time The Reds were the dominant force. Robbie Fowler and Stan Collymore both went close in the first five minutes, and it was only a matter of time before Liverpool made the breakthrough.

It came in the 19th minutes from a Stan Collymore 25-yarder. Ludek Miklosko got his finger tips to the ball, but it wasn't enough. Liverpool's second goal was scored by skipper John Barnes seven minutes before half time. Stan Collymore supplied the cross, Barnsey flicked the ball over Miklosko and into the net. It was his first goal since his double strike against Spurs in August.

Meanwhile, Newcastle were effectively blowing their title chances with a 2-1 defeat at Blackburn and Manchester United were consolidating their position with a 1-0 win at Coventry. Realistically, it now looked as though Liverpool would have to be content with third place.

John Barnes watchs as his shot goes in

Robbie on target yet again - this time he hits the equaliser in the local derby...leaving Neville Southall floudering in the Goodison Park mud

It was local derby day - the 154th - on 16 April, with the Reds' visit to EVERTON at Goodison Park. The Blue half of Merseyside dominated the first half, with Liverpool putting in a poor show. Everton opened the scoring on 19 minutes when Andrei Kanchelskis hammered home a John Ebbrell effort which had rebounded off the Liverpool crossbar.

The Reds were much improved in the second period. The chances began to come and Stan

No, it's not Spot the Ball - but some frantic local derby action against Everton!

Collymore struck the Everton crossbar. But the equaliser did not arrive until three minutes from time, when Robbie Fowler scored from close in, after a fine cross from the left by Stan Collymore.

In the 72nd minute Roy Evans had made a substitution, sending on Ian Rush in place of Neil Ruddock. It was to the great striker's last Merseyside derby.

Stan scores the only goal against Middlesbrough

Liverpool's last match in April brought Bryan Robson's MIDDLESBROUGH to Anfield. The Match Fax show that Liverpool won 1-0, with a Stan Collymore goal in the 70th minute, from a John Barnes pass. The result secured Liverpool a place in Europe for 1996-97.

But the match will always be remembered as Ian Rush's last apperance in a Liverpool shirt at Anfield (he came on as a sub for Robbie Fowler on the hour). And the 40,000+ fans gave him a rapturous and emotional farewell. Rushie has been one of Liverpool's most enduring stars and a world class goalscorer. He will be sorely missed at the club. He said afterwards "I wanted to stay on the pitch forever."

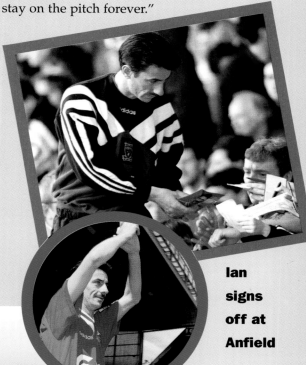

Ian signs off at Anfield

'Farewell Anfield'

MATCH FAX - APRIL 1996

Competition	Date	Venue	Attendance	Result
Prem	3.4	Anfield	40,702	Liverpool 4 Newcastle 3
Prem	6.4	Highfield Rd	23,137	Coventry 1 Liverpool 0
Prem	8.4	Anfield	40,326	Liverpool 2 West Ham 0
Prem	16.4	Goodison Pk	40,120	Everton 1 Liverpool 1
Prem	27.4	Anfield	40,782	Liverpool 1 Middlesbrough 0

Super REDS

MARK WRIGHT

FACT FILE
Name: Mark Wright
Birthdate: 1 August 1963
Birthplace: Dorchester
Height: 6' 3" Weight: 12st 11lbs
Previous clubs: Oxford United,
Southampton, Derby County
International:
England Under 21 & Full

STEVE HARKNESS

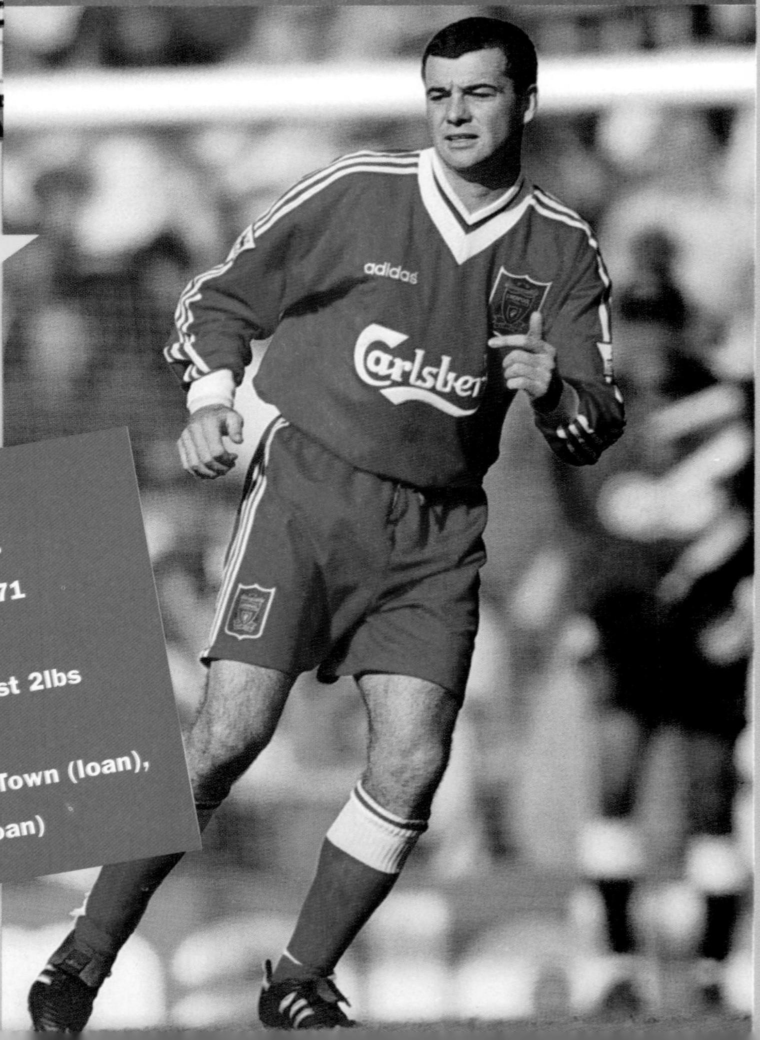

FACT FILE
Name: Steven Harkness
Birthdate: 27 August 1971
Birthplace: Carlisle
Height: 5' 10" Weight: 11st 2lbs
Previous clubs:
Carlisle United Huddersfield Town (loan),
Southend United (loan)

LIVERPOOL in 1995-96

Ian Rush scores his last goal for Liverpool, against Manchester City

Mayday saw Liverpool at Highbury for the Premiership clash with ARSENAL. It was a rather one-sided game, in which Arsenal defended well and Liverpool were poor. Once again keeper David James showed what a superb professional he is. In the closing thirty minutes he produced three world class saves to deny the Gunners who were hungry for that goal.

Thanks largely to James' acrobatic exploits, the points were shared.

Maine Road was the scene of Liverpool's last Premiership tussle of the season, against relegation-threatened MANCHESTER CITY. The Sky Blues fought desperately for Premiership survival. If they had won the match they would have stayed up. But in the event they found themselves 2-0 down at half time, to an unfortunate own goal by Steve Lomas on 6 minutes when he failed to deal with a Steve McManaman cross. Then, in the 40th minute Ian Rush fired home his last goal for Liverpool from 20-yards, and it looked as though it was all over for City.

The second half told a different tale. Man City fought back magnificently and managed to level the scored with goals from Uwe Rosler (a penalty) and Kit Symons. But it wasn't enough. The day's other results conspired to see City relegated on an inferior goal-difference.

Liverpool had finished in third place with 71 points, behind Champions Manchester United and runners-up Newcastle.

Now there was just one more match to look forward to...

David James saves against Manchester City

The FA Cup final, which pitted Liverpool against MANCHESTER UNITED at Wembley, promised to be a classic. Already Premier League Champions, United were looking to complete the League and FA Cup 'double' for the second time in the '90s. Liverpool, the most successful club in England and 'double' winners themselves in 1985-86, were determined to prevent history from being made.

The match proved a big disappointment. It was dominated by two sets of nerve-ridden players who failed to properly express themselves on the big stage.

David James had to be at his best after just five minutes when he was tested by a blistering shot from United's David Beckham. Five minutes later Stan Collymore almost got a shot on goal, but his effort was blocked by Phil Neville.

Stan was on target a minute later, shooting from an acute angle, but his shot was gathered by Peter Schmeichel. In the sixteenth minute the Liverpool defence stifled an attack by Andy Cole who had broken through with a clear chance to score.

Robbie Fowler attempted a header at goal in the 22nd minute, but the effort was ineffective, thanks to some pressurised United defending. Just before half time a Jamie Redknapp shot sailed high over the bar.

Things did not improve much in the second period. On 61 minutes Jamie Redknapp unleashed a terrific shot, but once again Peter Schmiechel made a good save. Two minutes later a John Scales header missed the target.

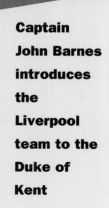

Captain John Barnes introduces the Liverpool team to the Duke of Kent

The Skippers shake on it!

In the 74th minute Stan Collymore was substituted by Ian Rush - making his last appearance in a Liverpool shirt. On 81 minutes Robbie Fowler attempted a lob which did not come off.

Then, in the 86th minute, disaster struck for Liverpool when David James' attempt to punch the ball clear, deflected off Ian Rush and fell into the path of Eric Cantona. The Frenchman took a step backwards and returned the ball through the defence and into the net.

It was the only goal of the game and it gave United that second 'double'. To say that the Liverpool players and fans were gutted is an understatement. But it makes them more determined than ever to get back on the glory trail in 1996-97.

John Barnes and Jamie Redknapp take on Ryan Giggs

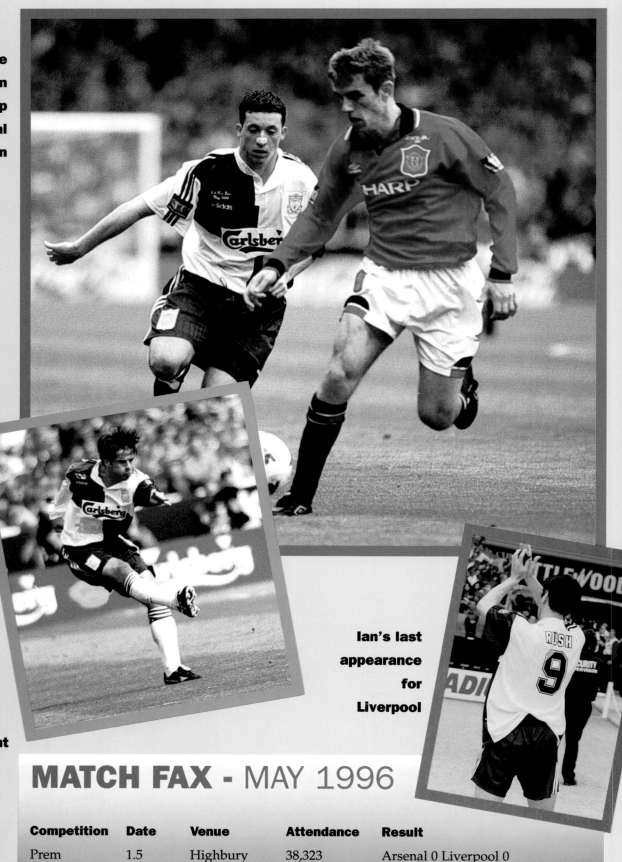

Robbie Fowler in FA Cup final action

A Jamie Redknapp effort which went over the bar

Ian's last appearance for Liverpool

MATCH FAX - MAY 1996

Competition	Date	Venue	Attendance	Result
Prem	1.5	Highbury	38,323	Arsenal 0 Liverpool 0
Prem	5.5	Maine Road	31,436	Manchester City 2 Liverpool 2
FAC final	11.5	Wembley	79,007	Manchester United 1 Liverpool 0

LIVERPOOL FACTS & FIGURES

1995-6 - FINAL PREMIER LEAGUE TABLE

	P	W	D	L	F	A	Pts
Manchester United	38	25	7	6	73	35	82
Newcastle United	38	24	6	8	66	37	78
LIVERPOOL	**38**	**20**	**11**	**7**	**70**	**34**	**71**
Aston Villa	38	18	9	11	52	35	63
Arsenal	38	17	12	9	49	32	63
Everton	38	17	10	11	64	44	61
Blackburn Rovers	38	18	7	13	61	47	61
Tottenham Hotspur	38	16	13	9	50	38	61
Nottingham Forest	38	15	13	10	50	54	58
West Ham United	38	14	9	15	43	52	51
Chelsea	38	12	14	12	46	44	50
Middlesbrough	38	11	10	17	35	50	43
Leeds United	38	12	7	19	40	57	43
Wimbledon	38	10	11	17	55	70	41
Sheffield Wednesday	38	10	10	18	48	61	40
Coventry City	38	8	14	16	42	60	38
Southampton	38	9	11	18	34	52	38
Manchester City	38	9	11	18	33	58	38
Queens Park Rangers	38	9	6	23	38	57	33
Bolton Wanderers	38	8	5	25	39	71	29

PREMIER LEAGUE GOALSCORERS

Robbie Fowler	28
Stan Collymore	14
Steve McManaman	6
Ian Rush	5
Neil Ruddock	5
Jamie Redknapp	3
John Barnes	3
Mark Wright	2
Steve Harkness	1
Michael Thomas	1
Own goals	2
Total	**70**

ANFIELD ATTENDANCES

Total	751,501
Average	39,552
Highest	40,820 v Chelsea
Lowest	34,063 v Wimbledon

FA CUP LIVERPOOL'S ROUTE TO WEMBLEY

Third Round	Liverpool	7	Rochdale	0
Fourth Round	Shrewsbury	0	Liverpool	4
Fifth Round	Liverpol	2	Chartlon	1
Sixth Round	Leeds	0	Liverpool	0
Sixth Rd Replay	Liverpool	3	Leeds	0
Semi-final	Aston Villa	0	Liverpool	3

FINAL LIVERPOOL 0 MANCHESTER UNITED 1